"Take Action" Expense Tracker

Belongs To

NAME: _______________________________

PHONE: _______________________________

Thanks for purchasing "Take Action Expense Tracker."

Get your finances on track. Expense tracking/logbook/planner is essential in our daily lives. Based on our experience while dealing with day-to-day expenses, this has been designed to track every penny to understand where our hard earn money goes and what costs need to be controlled. This tracker will give you a detailed analysis of you finances for the entire year by breaking up in Weeks, Months, Quarter and Year.

Whenever we get the chance to save, we would like to do that; sometimes, we spent money unnecessarily and later realized the money spent is not required or can be postpone. If we want to understand our finances, then tracking is a must. Every penny needs to track, analyze and then update the spending habit. There are many ways to do that, but many of us would like to pen down the spending and understand it on paper.

"Money is so crucial to our lives that every human being is trying to unfold the secret to manage our lives better. We'll take a skeptical look at money and explore where it fits into this universe."

How to use this tracker:
This tracker/planner has been designed for 52 weeks, four quarters, and 12 months. Every month has four pages per week, one monthly summary and notes, a comments page, one quarterly goal & commitments page.

1. **Quarterly Goals & Commitments:** Write all your financial goals and commitments for the quarter
2. **Week 1:** Record all your expenses and income for the week every day
3. **Week 2:** Record all your expenses and income for the week every day.
4. **Week 3:** Record all your expenses and income for the week every day
5. **Week 4**: Record all your expenses and income for the week every day
6. **Monthly Summary:** Here, you will document a financial summary for the month includes income, expenses, savings, and you will have the visibility for next month on where to spend, cut downs and improve savings
7. **Comments / Notes:** Write all your comments or notes for the month
8. **Yearly Summary:** Yearly summary with quarterly analysis, balance carry forward for next year

*"Don't forget to write down your goals for the
quarter and track effectively"*

Quarter 1 - Goals and Commitments

Financial Goals		
Sr. No.	Description	Amount

Financial Commitments		
Sr. No.	Description	Amount

Quarter 1

Month: ______________ Year: ____________ Checking / Cash Balance as of ______________

Date	Description	Expenses	Income	Balance
Total As Of ________________________				
Balance carry forward				

Week 1

Month: ___________ Year: ___________   Checking / Cash Balance as of ___________

Date	Description	Expenses	Income	Balance
Total As Of ___________________				
Balance carry forward				

Month: ______________ Year: ______________   Checking / Cash Balance as of ______________

Date	Description	Expenses	Income	Balance
Total As Of ______________________				
Balance carry forward				

Month: _____________ Year: ____________   Checking / Cash Balance as of ______________

Date	Description	Expenses	Income	Balance
Total As Of ________________________				
Balance carry forward				

Month: _____________ Year: ___________ Checking / Cash Balance as of ____________

Date	Description	Expenses	Income	Balance
Total As Of _____________________				
Balance carry forward				

Monthly Summary

Week	Description	Expenses	Income	Balance
1				
2				
3				
4				
	Total			

Saving Summary

Week	Description	Date	Deposit	Balance
1				
2				
3				
4				
		Total		

Month In Review

Week	Amount
Total Monthly Income	
Total Monthly Expense	
Total Monthly Saving	
Balance Carry Forward Amount For Next Month	

Notes / Comments / Improvements / Planning

Month: _____________Year: ___________   Checking / Cash Balance as of ____________

Date	Description	Expenses	Income	Balance
Total As Of ____________________				
Balance carry forward				

Week 1

Month: _____________ Year: ____________   Checking / Cash Balance as of _____________

Date	Description	Expenses	Income	Balance
Total As Of ____________________				
Balance carry forward				

Week 2

Month: ___________ Year: ___________   Checking / Cash Balance as of ___________

Date	Description	Expenses	Income	Balance
Total As Of ___________________				
Balance carry forward				

Week 3

Month: ____________Year: ____________ Checking / Cash Balance as of ____________

Date	Description	Expenses	Income	Balance
Total As Of ____________________				
Balance carry forward				

Week 4

Month: ____________ Year: ____________   Checking / Cash Balance as of ____________

Date	Description	Expenses	Income	Balance
Total As Of ____________________				
Balance carry forward				

Monthly Summary

Week	Description	Expenses	Income	Balance
1				
2				
3				
4				
	Total			

Saving Summary

Week	Description	Date	Deposit	Balance
1				
2				
3				
4				
		Total		

Month In Review

Week	Amount
Total Monthly Income	
Total Monthly Expense	
Total Monthly Saving	
Balance Carry Forward Amount For Next Month	

Notes / Comments / Improvements / Planning

Month: ______________ Year: ____________   Checking / Cash Balance as of ______________

Date	Description	Expenses	Income	Balance
Total As Of ______________________				
Balance carry forward				

Week 1

Month: _____________Year: ___________ Checking / Cash Balance as of ______________

Date	Description	Expenses	Income	Balance
Total As Of _______________________				
Balance carry forward				

Month: __________ Year: __________ Checking / Cash Balance as of __________

Date	Description	Expenses	Income	Balance
Total As Of _______________				
Balance carry forward				

Week 3

Month: _________ Year: _________   Checking / Cash Balance as of ___________

Date	Description	Expenses	Income	Balance
Total As Of _________________				
Balance carry forward				

Month: ___________ Year: __________ Checking / Cash Balance as of ___________

Date	Description	Expenses	Income	Balance
Total As Of ___________________				
Balance carry forward				

Monthly Summary

Week	Description	Expenses	Income	Balance
1				
2				
3				
4				
	Total			

Saving Summary

Week	Description	Date	Deposit	Balance
1				
2				
3				
4				
		Total		

Month In Review

Week	Amount
Total Monthly Income	
Total Monthly Expense	
Total Monthly Saving	
Balance Carry Forward Amount For Next Month	

Notes / Comments / Improvements / Planning

Quarterly Summary

Month	Description	Expenses	Income	Balance
	Total			

Saving Summary

Month	Description	Date	Deposit	Balance
		Total		

Quarter In Review

Description	Amount
Total Quarterly Income	
Total Quarterly Expense	
Total Quarterly Saving	
Balance Carry Forward Amount For Next Quarter	

Quarterly Planning / Improvements / Notes

Quarter 2 - Goals and Commitments

Financial Goals

Sr. No.	Description	Amount

Financial Commitments

Sr. No.	Description	Amount

Quarter 2

Month: ____________ Year: ____________ Checking / Cash Balance as of ____________

Date	Description	Expenses	Income	Balance
Total As Of ____________________				
Balance carry forward				

Week 1

Month: ___________ Year: ___________   Checking / Cash Balance as of ___________

Date	Description	Expenses	Income	Balance
Total As Of _____________________				
Balance carry forward				

Week 2

Month: ____________Year: ___________   Checking / Cash Balance as of ____________

Date	Description	Expenses	Income	Balance
Total As Of ________________				
Balance carry forward				

Week 3

Month: _____________ Year: ____________   Checking / Cash Balance as of ____________

Date	Description	Expenses	Income	Balance
Total As Of _____________________				
Balance carry forward				

Week 4

Month: ____________ Year: ___________   Checking / Cash Balance as of ____________

Date	Description	Expenses	Income	Balance
Total As Of ___________________				
Balance carry forward				

Monthly Summary

Week	Description	Expenses	Income	Balance
1				
2				
3				
4				
	Total			

Saving Summary

Week	Description	Date	Deposit	Balance
1				
2				
3				
4				
		Total		

Month In Review

Week	Amount
Total Monthly Income	
Total Monthly Expense	
Total Monthly Saving	
Balance Carry Forward Amount For Next Month	

Notes / Comments / Improvements / Planning

Month: ____________Year: ____________ Checking / Cash Balance as of ____________

Date	Description	Expenses	Income	Balance
Total As Of ____________________				
Balance carry forward				

Month: ___________ Year: ___________   Checking / Cash Balance as of ___________

Date	Description	Expenses	Income	Balance
Total As Of ___________________				
Balance carry forward				

Week 2

Month: _____________ Year: ___________ Checking / Cash Balance as of ____________

Date	Description	Expenses	Income	Balance
Total As Of ________________				
Balance carry forward				

Week 3

Month: _____________ Year: ____________ Checking / Cash Balance as of ___________

Date	Description	Expenses	Income	Balance
Total As Of ___________________				
Balance carry forward				

Month: ____________ Year: ____________ Checking / Cash Balance as of ____________

Date	Description	Expenses	Income	Balance
Total As Of ____________________				
Balance carry forward				

Monthly Summary

Week	Description	Expenses	Income	Balance
1				
2				
3				
4				
	Total			

Saving Summary

Week	Description	Date	Deposit	Balance
1				
2				
3				
4				
		Total		

Month In Review

Week	Amount
Total Monthly Income	
Total Monthly Expense	
Total Monthly Saving	
Balance Carry Forward Amount For Next Month	

Notes / Comments / Improvements / Planning

Month: _____________ Year: ___________ Checking / Cash Balance as of ______________

Date	Description	Expenses	Income	Balance
Total As Of ____________________				
Balance carry forward				

Week 1

Month: _____________Year: ___________   Checking / Cash Balance as of ____________

Date	Description	Expenses	Income	Balance
Total As Of ____________________				
Balance carry forward				

Week 2

Month: _________ Year: __________ Checking / Cash Balance as of ____________

Date	Description	Expenses	Income	Balance
Total As Of _______________________				
Balance carry forward				

Week 3

Month: _____________ Year: ____________   Checking / Cash Balance as of ____________

Date	Description	Expenses	Income	Balance
Total As Of ________________				
Balance carry forward				

Week 4

Month: ___________ Year: __________ Checking / Cash Balance as of ___________

Date	Description	Expenses	Income	Balance
Total As Of ___________________				
Balance carry forward				

Monthly Summary

Week	Description	Expenses	Income	Balance
1				
2				
3				
4				
	Total			

Saving Summary

Week	Description	Date	Deposit	Balance
1				
2				
3				
4				
		Total		

Month In Review

Week	Amount
Total Monthly Income	
Total Monthly Expense	
Total Monthly Saving	
Balance Carry Forward Amount For Next Month	

Notes / Comments / Improvements / Planning

Quarterly Summary

Month	Description	Expenses	Income	Balance
	Total			

Saving Summary

Month	Description	Date	Deposit	Balance
		Total		

Quarter In Review

Description	Amount
Total Quarterly Income	
Total Quarterly Expense	
Total Quarterly Saving	
Balance Carry Forward Amount For Next Quarter	

Quarterly Planning / Improvements / Notes

Quarter 3 - Goals and Commitments

Financial Goals		
Sr. No.	Description	Amount

Financial Commitments		
Sr. No.	Description	Amount

Quarter 3

Month: _____________ Year: ___________ Checking / Cash Balance as of ____________

Date	Description	Expenses	Income	Balance
Total As Of ____________________				
Balance carry forward				

Week 1

Month: ___________ Year: ___________ Checking / Cash Balance as of ___________

Date	Description	Expenses	Income	Balance
Total As Of ___________________				
Balance carry forward				

Week 2

Month: _____________Year: ____________ Checking / Cash Balance as of ____________

Date	Description	Expenses	Income	Balance
Total As Of ___________________				
Balance carry forward				

Week 3

Month: ____________ Year: ___________ Checking / Cash Balance as of ____________

Date	Description	Expenses	Income	Balance
Total As Of ____________________				
Balance carry forward				

Week 4

Month: _____________Year: ______________ Checking / Cash Balance as of ______________

Date	Description	Expenses	Income	Balance
Total As Of ______________________				
Balance carry forward				

Monthly Summary

Week	Description	Expenses	Income	Balance
1				
2				
3				
4				
	Total			

Saving Summary

Week	Description	Date	Deposit	Balance
1				
2				
3				
4				
		Total		

Month In Review

Week	Amount
Total Monthly Income	
Total Monthly Expense	
Total Monthly Saving	
Balance Carry Forward Amount For Next Month	

Notes / Comments / Improvements / Planning

Date	Description	Expenses	Income	Balance
Total As Of ___________________				
Balance carry forward				

Month: ___________ Year: ___________   Checking / Cash Balance as of ___________

Date	Description	Expenses	Income	Balance
Total As Of ___________________				
Balance carry forward				

Week 2

Month: ____________ Year: ___________   Checking / Cash Balance as of ______________

Date	Description	Expenses	Income	Balance
Total As Of ____________________				
Balance carry forward				

Month: _____________ Year: ____________ Checking / Cash Balance as of ____________

Date	Description	Expenses	Income	Balance
Total As Of _____________________				
Balance carry forward				

Month: _____________ Year: ___________ Checking / Cash Balance as of _____________

Date	Description	Expenses	Income	Balance
Total As Of _____________________				
Balance carry forward				

Monthly Summary

Week	Description	Expenses	Income	Balance
1				
2				
3				
4				
	Total			

Saving Summary

Week	Description	Date	Deposit	Balance
1				
2				
3				
4				
		Total		

Month In Review

Week	Amount
Total Monthly Income	
Total Monthly Expense	
Total Monthly Saving	
Balance Carry Forward Amount For Next Month	

Notes / Comments / Improvements / Planning

Month: ______________ Year: ____________ Checking / Cash Balance as of ____________

Date	Description	Expenses	Income	Balance
Total As Of _______________________				
Balance carry forward				

Week 1

Month: ______________Year: ____________   Checking / Cash Balance as of ______________

Date	Description	Expenses	Income	Balance
Total As Of ______________________				
Balance carry forward				

Week 2

Month: ___________ Year: __________   Checking / Cash Balance as of ____________

Date	Description	Expenses	Income	Balance
Total As Of ___________________				
Balance carry forward				

Week 3

Month: ____________ Year: ____________ Checking / Cash Balance as of ____________

Date	Description	Expenses	Income	Balance
Total As Of ____________________				
Balance carry forward				

Month: ____________Year: ___________ Checking / Cash Balance as of ______________

Date	Description	Expenses	Income	Balance
Total As Of ________________________				
Balance carry forward				

Monthly Summary

Week	Description	Expenses	Income	Balance
1				
2				
3				
4				
	Total			

Saving Summary

Week	Description	Date	Deposit	Balance
1				
2				
3				
4				
		Total		

Month In Review

Week	Amount
Total Monthly Income	
Total Monthly Expense	
Total Monthly Saving	
Balance Carry Forward Amount For Next Month	

Notes / Comments / Improvements / Planning

Quarterly Summary

Month	Description	Expenses	Income	Balance
	Total			

Saving Summary

Month	Description	Date	Deposit	Balance
		Total		

Quarter In Review

Description	Amount
Total Quarterly Income	
Total Quarterly Expense	
Total Quarterly Saving	
Balance Carry Forward Amount For Next Quarter	

Quarterly Planning / Improvements / Notes

Quarter 4 - Goals and Commitments

Financial Goals		
Sr. No.	Description	Amount

Financial Commitments		
Sr. No.	Description	Amount

Quarter 4

Month: ____________ Year: ___________   Checking / Cash Balance as of ____________

Date	Description	Expenses	Income	Balance
Total As Of ______________________				
Balance carry forward				

Week 1

Month: ____________ Year: ___________ Checking / Cash Balance as of ___________

Date	Description	Expenses	Income	Balance
Total As Of ___________________				
Balance carry forward				

Week 2

Month: ______________ Year: ____________   Checking / Cash Balance as of ____________

Date	Description	Expenses	Income	Balance
Total As Of _______________			
Balance carry forward			

Week 3

Month: _____________ Year: ____________   Checking / Cash Balance as of ____________

Date	Description	Expenses	Income	Balance
Total As Of ______________________				
Balance carry forward				

Month: ___________ Year: ___________   Checking / Cash Balance as of ___________

Date	Description	Expenses	Income	Balance
Total As Of ___________________				
Balance carry forward				

Monthly Summary

Week	Description	Expenses	Income	Balance
1				
2				
3				
4				
	Total			

Saving Summary

Week	Description	Date	Deposit	Balance
1				
2				
3				
4				
		Total		

Month In Review

Week	Amount
Total Monthly Income	
Total Monthly Expense	
Total Monthly Saving	
Balance Carry Forward Amount For Next Month	

Month: _____________Year: ___________ Checking / Cash Balance as of ____________

Date	Description	Expenses	Income	Balance
Total As Of _________________				
Balance carry forward				

Week 1

Month: ____________Year: ____________ Checking / Cash Balance as of ____________

Date	Description	Expenses	Income	Balance
Total As Of ________________				
Balance carry forward				

Week 2

Month: _____________ Year: ___________   Checking / Cash Balance as of ____________

Date	Description	Expenses	Income	Balance
Total As Of ___________________				
Balance carry forward				

Month: ___________ Year: ___________ Checking / Cash Balance as of ___________

Date	Description	Expenses	Income	Balance
Total As Of ___________________				
Balance carry forward				

Week 4

Month: _____________ Year: ___________   Checking / Cash Balance as of _____________

Date	Description	Expenses	Income	Balance
Total As Of _________________________				
Balance carry forward				

Monthly Summary

Week	Description	Expenses	Income	Balance
1				
2				
3				
4				
	Total			

Saving Summary

Week	Description	Date	Deposit	Balance
1				
2				
3				
4				
		Total		

Month In Review

Week	Amount
Total Monthly Income	
Total Monthly Expense	
Total Monthly Saving	
Balance Carry Forward Amount For Next Month	

Notes / Comments / Improvements / Planning

Month: _____________ Year: ___________   Checking / Cash Balance as of _______________

Date	Description	Expenses	Income	Balance
Total As Of ___________________				
Balance carry forward				

Week 1

Month: ____________ Year: ____________ Checking / Cash Balance as of ____________

Date	Description	Expenses	Income	Balance
Total As Of ____________________				
Balance carry forward				

Week 2

Month: ______________Year: ______________ Checking / Cash Balance as of ______________

Date	Description	Expenses	Income	Balance
Total As Of ______________				
Balance carry forward				

Week 3

Month: ___________ Year: ___________   Checking / Cash Balance as of ___________

Date	Description	Expenses	Income	Balance
Total As Of _________________				
Balance carry forward				

Week 4

Month: ____________ Year: ____________   Checking / Cash Balance as of ____________

Date	Description	Expenses	Income	Balance
Total As Of ____________________				
Balance carry forward				

Monthly Summary

Week	Description	Expenses	Income	Balance
1				
2				
3				
4				
	Total			

Saving Summary

Week	Description	Date	Deposit	Balance
1				
2				
3				
4				
		Total		

Month In Review

Week	Amount
Total Monthly Income	
Total Monthly Expense	
Total Monthly Saving	
Balance Carry Forward Amount For Next Month	

Quarterly Summary

Month	Description	Expenses	Income	Balance
	Total			

Saving Summary

Month	Description	Date	Deposit	Balance
		Total		

Quarter In Review

Description	Amount
Total Quarterly Income	
Total Quarterly Expense	
Total Quarterly Saving	
Balance Carry Forward Amount For Next Quarter	

Quarterly Planning / Improvements / Notes

Yearly Summary

Quarter	Description	Expenses	Income	Balance
	Total			

Saving Summary

Quarter	Description	Date	Deposit	Balance
		Total		

Year In Review

Description	Amount
Total Yearly Income	
Total Yearly Expense	
Total Yearly Saving	
Balance Carry Forward Amount For Next Year	

Summary of Year - Notes, Improvement or Planning for Next Year

Happy Saving
Happy Living